BESIDE MY EQUAL

By Alex Chornyj

Illustrated by Bella De Dios M

Cyberwit.net
HIG 45 Kaushambi Kunj, Kalindipuram
Allahabad - 211011 (U.P.) India
http://www.cyberwit.net
Tel: +(91) 9415091004
E-mail: info@cyberwit.net

Printed at Repro India Limited.

This book is dedicated to the two stars in my universe

Bella y Luna

Toby was ready willing and able to embark upon a new expedition as the adrenaline was at an all time high in him. The inspiration was present, but so was the reality of having to return to school.

After living through this adventure, he wasn't quite ready to assume an old, dull routine. This was not even remotely possible with Adrienne living so close by. She would be attending his school in the same grade. It was as if this had been written in the stars. Imagine having such a destiny unfolding before your very eyes! Coming back down to earth was somewhat cushioned by the fact of her mere presence. This spoke volumes about her impact on his consciousness.

They were two peas in the same pod. There was a dazzling in his aura whenever she was near. The same can be said of Toby's effect on Adrienne as well. She was like a jitterbug on a lake, vibrating and jumping about.

Toby's initial cosmic transformation display to Adrienne was a spectacular performance. She, of course, was filled in on the necessity of discretion with this knowledge. Under no circumstances was she to share such delicate information with other humans. This was the first lesson Stan Tress taught them. There was a danger present in releasing such life-altering realizations to the public. A need for caution served to avoid future complications in interactions with man. Adrienne was touched deeply by Toby feeling confident he could trust her with his secret.

The two of them tried to figure out how and why their lives had become inseparable. Their parents were simply mystified by this sudden blossoming friendship. Toby and Adrienne spent many waking hours filling in the gaps – of which there were few. It appeared there were forces at work with karmic intentions but who or what intelligent entities were behind this chemistry remained unknown.

Adrienne, having heard Toby's entire rendition of his fascinating journey, was enthralled by its uniqueness. She still wanted the missing link that would enlighten her about the source of her connection to him. They both finally came to the conclusion that trying to force an answer was not the right approach. When this intuition was meant to appear it had to have an unprovoked natural course. With their minds made up, this free flow of wispy energy through a telling channel only furthered their cause.

As they released from their complementing dreams, an anticipation of remarkable experiences was on a nearing horizon. The lavender hues which adorned these walls were warming to both of their hearts. There was a recognition on both of their parts that they were living and breathing their true purpose. Where this would take them was not yet revealed. If their previous rendezvous was any indication, they were in for untold wonders. No one knew what was right around the corner.

The winds of change had acted as a magnet, drawing two people with identical qualities into their inner realms. To look in a mirror was to see themselves in the other person. It was kind of unusual but, given the circumstances this vibrant energy had a gravitational pull to it. Each succeeding day brought them closer together. A means to an end – but they were at the very beginning. There was a hunger in their eyes as they came upon an enlightening moment. What they needed to understand was that lives of illumination were entering their minds through invisible channels.

There was still a week before school began so, basically, all of their free time was spent with each other.

On one particular morning, Toby and Adrienne planned an outing to explore around a lake that had a pristine waterfall. Water had not only a calming effect, but a soothing one as well.

Parents on both sides agreed to let them go as this place was near enough to ride their bicycles.

After Toby's infinite independent adventures this was a mere drop in the bucket, or was it? The most innocent of paths can, at times, reveal more than is expected.

Off they went with all the necessities – food, water, compass, jackets and hiking boots. Their instincts were stronger the closer they neared to their destination.

For their age of 10, both were rather mature and responsible. They knew full well not to approach a mother bear with cubs. One altercation with a bruin earlier that summer was sufficient to convince them to heed such warnings.

No such animals were seen from the ground so Toby, with Adrienne in agreement, found a secluded spot and uttered the word 'kwah'.

Instantly, he became a hawk, taking to the sky to do a search of the entire area. The freedom Toby felt was out of this world. The air beneath his wings was an emotional and uplifting exercise. His scan showed the forest contained no such fur-bearing creature.

Toby was following along a stream that led to the lake when he spotted a shiny object in the water.

His first thought was that it might make a good present for Adrienne so, down he went as if he were in pursuit of a fish.

Toby's whole body started to tingle so he knew something was up.

As he went underwater to retrieve the sparkling orb he saw, plain as day, it was in the shape of a horn. He was so excited by his find as the energy it emitted was pulsating. It was a peaceful telling piece.

Toby flew with this multi-coloured stone back upstream to where he was near to Adrienne. He said the word hawk and transformed back to his human body.

Before he returned to Adrienne he preformed a cleansing ritual Stan Tress had taught him.

He first ran it underwater and said, "I transform your negative energies into positive energies and then I re-energize you."

Toby then dedicated the crystal to Adrienne in goodness, white light, divine love and sound.

Lastly, he programmed it for Adrienne for great health, peace, love, light, harmony and synchronicity.

The stone now literally came alive and, before Toby reached Adrienne, he heard a scream.

He ran as fast as he could to where she was. Adrienne told Toby she felt a sharp, burning pain on her right shoulder just a moment before. Adrienne said the hurting was gone but, when Toby told her his story of the gem they both figured the two were somehow connected.

She held the stone in her hand and, just as Toby had felt this before, Adrienne now experienced waves of wavelengths.

Adrienne asked Toby to look at her right shoulder and when he did he saw an emblem in the shape of a horn. When she heard this Adrienne almost fainted.

Toby called for Stan Tress to appear and Stan was there in a jiffy. Stan explained to both of them that this was all part of Adrienne's evolution to becoming Toby's equal.

Adrienne was reassured by Stan and by the knowledge that the answers her and Toby were looking for were now at hand. There was no danger but Adrienne would now be able to transform into the forms that Toby could.

Now that this inquiry had its response, it was like a weight was lifted from their shoulders.

Stan spent the rest of the day with his two friends and they agreed the next logical step was for Adrienne to attempt shape shifting.

There was no better time than the present!

To say the least, this was a turning point in young Adrienne's life.

She uttered, at the same moment as Toby, the word 'KWAH' and magically they both became hawks. In the first seconds she struggled a bit to get used to being a hawk but she was highly adaptive.

"Am I really able to be what you are, Toby?" she asked.

"By the looks of it, yes you are, my fine feathered friend," insisted Toby.

Just like when Toby had his first day changing forms, Adrienne had to be steady as she goes.

Stan watched over them but Toby was now her tutor and it was an afternoon unlike any other Adrienne had ever been a part of.

Toby would perform a manoeuvre and then she would follow suit. She paid close attention to speed and angles. Adrienne also noticed how her vision and hearing had vastly improved. School had begun earlier than she expected.

Her teacher was patient, empathetic and thorough in his lesson. The door opened and a transformation shone a promising path. It was a day that these two never wanted to end as the possibilities were now infinite.

The symbol on her shoulder would be a permanent reminder of a purpose that has been revealed in all of its splendour. Her favourite rite of passage was the swooping motion as she found the gushes of air in a downward dive to be exhilarating.

How wonderful it was that this day came to pass.

It was evident Adrienne was a natural as she didn't miss a beat. From one movement to the other, she grew by leaps and bounds. There was a beauty and rhythmic flow in each artistic measure.

"It is hard to believe I have made this through in one piece," shared Adrienne.

"It is your commitment to detail which is your greatest strength," related Toby.

They could have gone on and on but Stan interrupted them near dusk.

"I think you two better high tail it back home before Adrienne's parents start to worry – and please remember, mum is the word," suggested Stan.

The day had run its full course faster than they would have liked.

Adrienne had her special crystal which felt like it had a life of its own.

She already had an idea to have it made into a chain. It was almost exactly like, certainly very similar to the one that Toby always wore.

They were like two bookends, but in a good way. This day served to uncover a few stones that had, until then, hidden their meanings.

With grace and gratitude, they were poised and ready for whatever would come next. It would be difficult to try to match the magic of the moment that these two found on this afternoon.

This was especially true for Adrienne who passed through a tunnel with flying colours. They came out the other side like shimmering rainbows. On the way home they couldn't stop talking or thinking about what tomorrow would bring.

Adrienne's parents heard all the stories about the excursion. They trusted Toby and as well they had grown fond of him.

Adrienne's dreams that night were full of adventure. They were an extension from the day's rapid rise. Trying to top that would be a major feat. It's not every day when a person learns of treasures for personal growth as she did. The chest was only briefly opened, but of what trinkets Adrienne saw, she was completely mesmerized by.

Her parents were amazed about the etching on their daughter's right shoulder. It was not man made and occurring naturally this horn was seen as a good omen.

All throughout the night, Toby and Adrienne communicated by a form of telepathy or a sharing of thoughts. They had become linked together on all levels. It was similar to being joined at the hip like a set of twins. They could bounce ideas back and forth without saying a word.

The morning brought a new dawn with a bright, positive vibration. The magic from the previous day formed these colourful striations in the sky. They had a ripple effect from being teased by a morning breeze.

Standing outside, Toby felt a heightened sensation even after all that he had endured.

Adrienne was there in an instant. She, too, was now on a parallel latitude with Toby. She looked at him the same moment he was staring into her eyes.

There was this energy bouncing back and forth between them in a circular pattern. They were definitely in their own little universe in an orbit whose purpose was to bring them face to face and heart to heart.

To them, the world was full of enchantment. Each moment was precious and, even at their tender age, these kids had their heads on straight. Their priorities were from a more mature point as they were sharp to catch onto what most children of their age group could not. This was a compliment to their very nature which displayed an understanding beyond their years.

With this in mind they took this morning to think of how, with their abilities, they could help the less fortunate. By being given these gifts, there was a responsibility to use them in a way that would bring benefit to not only themselves.

One thing both Toby and Adrienne noticed was how other animals now treated them. They could communicate with any wildlife they encountered. So the plan was to approach the principal from their school with the idea to start a program that promoted interaction between students and animals.

It was genius in its simplicity. The idea was that kids would develop a respect and kindness with earth's creatures and an additional result would be the creation of bonds between them from looking at each other differently.

When they informed their parents of this proposal, it was seen as a natural extension of themselves. In time, Adrienne's parents may be told of her new-found abilities but the present was, as of yet, too soon.

The idea they pitched was not a show and tell format but as real a living experience as possible. This meant going into the forest to see how animals were in their natural environments. Their routines of daily activities would provide a glimpse into the window of acquiring knowledge. To see how parents cared for their young, how they searched for food, how they built their homes, how infant animals playing together learned valuable life survival skills. This all, when put together, made a complete picture of the life and times of a particular species.

All grades could be involved in this proposed program, Toby and Adrienne said. Younger grades could have more brief encounters due to their shorter attention spans while the older grades could be involved on deeper levels to expand their horizons.

When this was explained to the principal, it was seen as a valuable teaching tool. It could serve to not only provide clearer insight into the essentials of daily living, but there was the side benefit for their friends in the forest. It was the last part that sold the value of this initiative.

Toby and Adrienne's sincere motive to reconnect kids to nature was seen as a win for all.

Safety was addressed and whenever one of these excursions was planned, Toby and Adrienne would lead the groups. They displayed character which would not be expected from two ordinary ten-year-olds.

The board of education had to study all of the aspects of this proposal to see if they would approve it on a limited basis so a trial run was given the go ahead.

Change is a normal part of life and those with the ability to adapt will survive. This proposed change offered to place the classroom in the field where nature would then assume the role of instructor.

It was then a waiting game to see if it would be approved and work. But, either way, the presentation placed these two on a level of high achievers.

What they were actually attempting to do was share what they had only recently learned – animals had a normal fear of humans and this could begin a turn to the better to see each other in a different light. This would not happen overnight, but in small, consistent steps improvement would be realized.

Much could be said about the aura of energy stream that surrounds each life-form and acts like a protective coating as does the earth's atmosphere. If a person is of the light and kind, this would be a sign to children and creatures by way of seeing the warmth and colour coming from their circular flow.

There is an innocence of the heart in the young and in animals which creates an awareness with a higher vision to see such invisible traits. As we get older, most lose this ability due to the pressures and stress of life. By practising deep breathing and meditation, this sixth sense can be kept. If you don't use it, this part of who we are fades away.

The part which no teachers or youngsters could see was the animal side of Toby and Adrienne. There was an instant recognition when these two neared only wildlife as to their true alter-identities. What was hidden to humans was revealed clear as day to other forms of life.

This connection or bond was a strength in all aspects of contact. A silent communication through the use of shared thoughts between creatures and the two of them let it be known what their purpose and peaceful intentions were. No one was above or below the other but, as equals along one flat plane. This was all about opening up horizons that forever had been closed due to a lack of understanding.

As word of Toby's good deeds were passed from when he was a whale, the same was now true for what he and Adrienne were doing. From this came new hope and promise in the forests that the light at the end of the tunnel was beginning to shine.

The first excursion for a class was escorted by Toby, Adrienne and two teachers. As if this was a rehearsed beforehand, a hawk from its nest high atop a tree swooped down upon them.

"Look out," said one of the teachers.

"Please watch as I feel no danger," Toby returned.

He put out his left arm and the bird gently landed on his arm without causing a scratch. Toby secretly let the bird know what he wanted it to do.

The bird nestled its head against him soft as a feather. This drew reactions of disbelief from all in attendance, except for Adrienne.

They were putting on a show but still wanting to be responsible in letting all involved learn to develop their instincts. If they had not known otherwise, this would have appeared to be Toby's pet. The hawk flew back to its nest then next dove down and followed along a river.

One of the teachers caught this on camera.

The fellow did a funny thing, entering the water then returning to fly around Toby and Adrienne, flapping its wings and getting them both rather wet. As if this wasn't enough, he then landed on the ground beside Adrienne, leaving a small jade-like stone right at her feet. This was seen as a peace offering to which the kids were in awe. The hawk then flew off back to its nest. The children all wanted to hold the sparkling emerald-like orb.

Adrienne informed them that she first wished to cleanse the stone. She went to the river and dunked it in the water saying, "I transform your negative energies into positive energies and then I re-energize you."

Adrienne then showed each child that, after holding it, the stone had to be blown on to remove the vibrations imprinted from the last holder. This prevented one person from passing their energy onto the next one in line. It was explained that in such frequency waves people carry ailments and infections which can then be transmitted to others if this cleansing is not used.

It was an eye-opening experience for all involved. Upon returning to the school, the older students were asked to put pen to paper to record what happened that day.

There were small differences in their stories as each person is an individual. The overall common theme was this creation of a deeper understanding of nature. The underlying chord was a connection between humans and the surrounding life forms.

This was just one outing but it was a bright beginning. The sharing of this information the next day at school made for a close-knit group. The parents of these children were equally surprised by the positive responses.

There had been some doubt in the back of parents' minds as to what may happen with visiting such an insecure place. But students knew from talks with teachers that, if a danger was felt during one of these walks, the adults would enact safety measures.

Each teacher wore a whistle only to used in an emergency situation to notify all of a problem. An air horn to be used to ward off any aggressive animals was brought along. First aid kits and cell phones were also part of the emergency plan. You could never be too prepared with it came to the responsibility of the well-being of each child.

There was room to grow, improve, develop and learn from each successive trip. One built upon the other to answer questions from inquiring pupils. The purpose from the get go was to see all sides from differing angles to form a clearer picture of interactions with nature.

This became a very successful program and, with glitches ironed out, as they presented themselves.

Overall impressions changed from somewhat skeptical at the start to a more rounded, clearer sense of how each fit in the other's world. There were good and bad apples in every barrel, but this taught the children not to paint each with the same brush.

Pre-judging is not acceptable as this leads to slanted views, they learned. An open mind looks at each situation based on the objective eyes of the seer. To observe for themselves was a much truer, more

reliable teacher than rumours based on unproven theory. These near-to-nature experiences were what the doctor ordered to narrow the gap of understanding between the animals and humans.

Awareness and respect were the focus of these rendezvous to resurrect a bridge that had long fallen apart. Now the two parts met in the middle, finding common ground. This bodes well for the future and coming generations if a closeness is kept moving towards each other, thought Toby and Adrienne.

Toby, in a dream one night, had an awakening moment about Adrienne's parents. They were often saying how much time these two spent together. It was time to spill the beans about what was transpiring. Holding this secret was a difficult task and, like Toby's parents, there was disbelief until they witnessed with their very eyes.

Toby and Adrienne spoke to her mother and father but they, at first, thought this was a game.

A day was set for a demonstration at Lake Quilling and reality was about to strike home. Toby's parents were present as well, as a means of support.

"Are we really doing this?" asked Adrienne's father.

"Yes, we most certainly are," replied Adrienne. The whole process had been first explained in detail. Toby uttered the word 'kwah' and, just like before, he became a hawk.

Just as quickly, Adrienne said the word 'kwah' and she, too, transformed into a hawk.

Adrienne's mother fainted and when she came to there was a realization on her parents' part that their world had changed.

There was much conversation about what this all meant. One thing for sure is that Toby and Adrienne were two special people drawn together by fate.

The necessity of secrecy was again put forward. This sharing of information all came about due to Toby and Adrienne's evolution. They were rising higher and a plan was in place to achieve even greater aspirations.

His whole adventure was told to Adrienne's parents. They couldn't believe what they were hearing.

Their successful project with students at their school in introducing them to the other side of nature led them to their next logical step. Toby and Adrienne decided they wished to create a huge open expanse where all wildlife was free of being hunted by man. This was going to take an enormous investment to make this dream a reality.

On that note, Toby reminded his parents of the ship he had safely hidden off the coast of Africa. But it was one thing to have a treasure and another to quietly convert this into ready-to-use currency. Whenever Toby was in doubt, Stan Tress would appear and this time was no different.

"Toby, I have a friend who was involved with the sale of items recently when we released all of the ancient sea galleons back to the surface from the underwater volcano in the Bermuda Triangle," said Stan.

"His name is Dixon Chartier and he would be willing to assist you in your selfless endeavour free of charge."

Stan went on to tell Toby that Dixon had a company based in the Bahamas that dealt with rare antiquities. Stan contacted Dixon, relaying all of the information and it was agreed that the entire ship and its precious valuables would be towed by Toby, Adrienne and Stan beneath the ocean's surface from the hidden cove beside the African coast to Dixon's warehouse complex under the invisibility of night.

As the school year was again nearing an end, they had one month to prepare for this daunting task at hand. First things were first so a practice rehearsal was set after both sets of parents approved.

Toby was able to safely locate the ship using memory reminders he left in place the first time he was there.

Adrienne proved she was a great swimmer as a whale as well.

The three of them spent time travelling from Africa to the Bahamas. They made it in just over a day testing out their abilities. From this trip, they were able to determine that they should take a little over two days to complete this journey. The plan was finalized with a date in two weeks at the end of June. There was an excitement to all of this commotion but they had to be well rested and nourished to accomplish this feat.

When they were with the ship the first time, Toby had secured three strong tow lines that could easily be used by three whales. Nothing was left to chance. There were going to be enough surprises along the way to make the journey challenging.

On the morning they were leaving, the three of them met at Lake Quilling. Their parents felt safe in the fact that Stan Tress was going to be with them every step of the way.

Each spoke the word 'kwah' and they were off flying to the east coast of Canada. This was a stretch to last about two days. Time was important but their safety was even more so.

The weather was fair and favourable to help them reach their first destination. Along the way they would stop to nibble on fresh fish and drink water. Adrienne liked to be able to speak in the language of a hawk with her two friends. These were all a bunch of firsts for Adrienne who was finding her new self more with each passing day. A voyage of discovery was unearthing these realizations which were filling in the blanks according to a telling wind. The breeze upon which they were flying was whistling a tune that the three of them instinctively knew. It was a sound whose vibration just matched the beauty of this shimmering sun.

Adrienne did not question why this all came to be as it felt like fate was etching them into a pursuit of happiness. The feeling of freedom when up in the sky just took each of their breaths away.

They came across other birds who wished to join them but this was not their purpose. A kind word and a polite 'no thank you' was all that could be offered.

As they neared the ocean waters their senses picked up on the scent of salt in the air. They rested in a forest for the night, close by the Atlantic Ocean. It was a quiet place where they wouldn't attract attention in the morning.

As first light, they changed back into human form and just as quickly the word 'elahw' was spoken while out in the water and they all transformed into whales.

A breakfast of fish was what the doctor ordered to start the next leg of their journey.

There was now this anticipation in their every movement. They swam with grace and dignity in time with one another. They could taste the shores of Africa as each had a hunger to see this challenge through to its successful completion.

As with other hawks, once other whales got a whiff of what was taking place, they too wanted in. A respectful decline was given as it was explained that this was a mission of mercy and not a fun-filled expedition. The cold, hard truth was necessary in order to wake these cling-ons about the serious nature of this intention. There were dangers every step of the way but it was flattering how many whales wished to be part of this. It was like this beam of light with a lavender hue was shielding them from any potential harm. The ocean was filled with the good and the bad so such a warmth, although unexpected, was received with gratitude. Time passed as it usually does when one was as busy as they were. One driving thought was to get where they were going without enduring any harm.

The sea turtles and dolphins were curious, but the only attention unwanted was that of man. There was an underwater current that seemed to help them reach their destination a little faster. An inner beacon acted like a compass to keep them on track and on pace. Toby was as determined as Stan and Adrienne to reach the ship safely. The sights they saw while swimming were memorable, indeed. There was one spot where they came upon some ruins. They did not stop due to the need to push on but all three of them felt the vibrational pull of this special place.

"We will return here when we are not in such a rush," said Stan.

The surroundings had all the marks of a mystical palace. There was a barrier which hid it from the outside world but, for some reason, they had been allowed to observe its presence.

An arch was clearly visible and, what gave Toby a sense of deja vu, were the three symbols carved into its surface. They were in the shape of three horned moons.

Adrienne had no idea what caused Toby to stir but Stan sure did.

"Just like on the planet of Nroh, eh Toby," Stan smiled.

"All of these journeys are connected together by spirit," exclaimed Toby.

Toby and Stan relayed what this all meant to Adrienne who caught on rather quickly.

An even deeper intuition came to light as Toby saw each one of them being tied to one of the moons.

This gravitational pull was increasing in its polarity. Toby remembered what the purple unicorn said about him being their protector and, if ever his horn's colour changed from violet, then he was to return at once to Nroh to help.

Thankfully, Toby thought that the horn he wore on a chain around his neck was still purple.

Each event was falling into place lining up as would a constellation in the night sky. It almost felt like this as a path that was already written into a living script which they were pursuing. The longer this went on,

the stronger became this inclination. Enough time was spent dwelling on what would happen when, not if, they returned to this sacred place. This intention was added to their bucket to do list.

Their current train of thought saw them resume their course as time was of the essence to maintain their somewhat schedule. It was only another five hours of heading east that brought them to where the ship was located. All of the tow lines were inspected and everything seemed ready to go.

It was agreed upon that a rest was in order so a good days sleep was to be had. By the first sign of dusk, they were off to be hidden by the dark. They didn't want to attract any onlookers in this mission of mercy. This is exactly what it was to acquire an island not inhabited by man and off the beaten path.

Their internal clocks were all on the same page, so to speak. It was like they could all read each other's thoughts which, at a critical moment, could be a life saving gift. Each pulled their own weight equally in this difficult task to get the vessel swiftly and safely to a concealed port in the Bahamas where Dixon Chartier was expecting them.

They stayed many thousand feet below the surface where it was all as black as two pieces of coal.

The sights with all the dormant volcanoes and infinite valleys made for quite the scenes to pass time with. Before they knew it, they were near their final target. The ship had held itself together throughout the entire trip quite well.

Stan could feel the oneness developing between Toby and Adrienne. It was hard for Stan to see any difference between the two of them. This closeness was fulfilling another part of the process, that being the creation of a dynamic, enduring bond between Toby and Adrienne. In a short period of time, two virtual strangers became life-long, close-knit friends. Where their relationship was heading, only time would tell.

Dixon Chartier had installed special lights as the three were approaching at night. The lights would act like landing lights on a runway for planes. This made a difficult task somewhat easier to finish. Dixon used the same three tow lines to guide the ancient piece of history into its berth in his main warehouse.

Other than thousands of barnacles attached to the bottom, the ship had proven to be seaworthy under the direction of the three blue whales. It was an experience for the ages kept under a cloak of secrecy to ward off any would be pirates who would want to pry this treasure from them.

Once the ship was placed in dry dock, the building was secured as tight as a drum. Stan, Toby and Adrienne changed back to human form by speaking the word whale. Dixon was amazed by the miracle of this transformation as it looked like something out of a science fiction movie.

There were cabins on the property where all could rest for the night. Morning would come soon enough when the real work would begin with the cataloguing of each item. This turned out to be a restless sleep for all as their anticipation of what they would find was through the roof.

The dreams they had that night were vivid and bridged the gap between fantasy and reality. They were living a dream by what they had touched in their last few days. Their horizons and belief systems were evolving and adapting to a higher awareness that was altering what they knew was possible and true.

With the new dawn came a light which reflected a revealing ray.

First thing in the morning Toby and Adrienne contacted their parents to let them know they were fine. They all had a delicious breakfast of fruits and juices. It turned out the ship was from Spain, constructed in the year 1558. She had been christened after her ill-fated captain's daughter and named La Luna.

Captain Majorca had three daughters, the oldest of which was Luna. There were, again, three moons on the stern with the ship's name, La Luna. The significance of this did not escape anyone. The theme from the beginning of Toby's adventures was the three ringing moons of Nroh. These constant reminders were making indentations upon everyone's consciousness.

A good place to start seemed to be the captain's quarters. Inside this room were the memories of a good man and a loving father. A ship's log was found which Stan and Dixon were able to understand.

The log was well-preserved, hidden inside an airtight chamber. The lost record detailed a devastating storm. This torrid storm was the reason why La Luna came to her fateful finish. Captain Majorca had gone down with the sinking ship as was the tradition and expectation in the days when accidents happened.

Underneath this log was another document which listed the ship's cargo item by item. This was a pleasant surprise, one which made their work less of a headache. La Luna was on an exploration and trading voyage when she became the victim of torrential seas. The crew had fought bravely, but the hole in her broadside was one problem they could not overcome. Their lives and dreams were snuffed out in a downward-suctioning whirlpool. This ship had rested for what seemed like an eternity until Toby first found her. This was the history La Luna which they came to know.

There seemed to be a jiggle when Toby placed this chamber back down on a wooden table.

"I think there may be something else hidden inside," Toby said.

He found a release button on the bottom which revealed a secret compartment in a false bottom. There was a sparkling glitter which came from the jewellery piece he found there. It was studded with diamonds on its edges and had a navy-blue enamel underlay in the shape of a heart. It had a 'T' in the upper left corner and an 'A' in the bottom right corner.

Toby and Adrienne picked up on this right away. There were also three tiny silver horns in the middle, separating the two letters. The mystery deepened as Toby and Adrienne realized this piece of jewellery was from 500 years before they were born. It was too specific to be a coincidence.

When each held it in their hands they both had visions of long ago in another life. It appeared to them that they were involved in a romance in the days of chivalry. If Toby and Adrienne hadn't figured it out before, the energy turned on the light perfectly, now. They were still very young but they looked at each other with a warming affection.

Stan, of course, knew by his intuition that this was going to happen. There was a distinct change as if this one step was equal to about ten such motions. They had their whole lives ahead of them. The two of them were following a fate of a destiny that was hot on their trails. Either way, this was going to be a story for the ages.

When Toby and Adrienne got caught up and came back down to earth, you could have heard a pin drop. Going forward there was a knowingness now shared between the two of them. A deeper sense of understanding now replaced their former shallow surface layer. A smile and wink were all that was needed to seal the deal.

"We better get back to the task at hand," reminded Adrienne.

Everything in the captains quarters was carefully catalogued. There were swords, fancy rings and an assortment of gold plates to itemize. Once this room was completed they were off to the cargo holds to list the inventory of these treasures. This took the better part of four days.

In such time they found gold, silver, diamonds, plates and a trove of valuable coins. By the time they were finished an approximate value was given that boggled their minds. Each person of the group was able to claim five trinkets for themselves. Toby and Adrienne's most cherished piece was the first one they found in the captain's room. They agreed to share this between themselves. It was like bringing two waves together which joined as one.

With an amount required to purchase a deserted island in the Bahamas for their purposes, a portion of the treasure was auctioned off privately. It was a stroke of luck on Toby's first adventure that secured this ship when he was a whale. To have a sanctuary for as many animals as possible was a dream come true. Plans were in the works as this island was purchased with the proceeds from the silent sale.

There was still at least three-quarters of the bounty untouched. This was converted into cash through quiet, anonymous market exchanges. The excess currency was placed in the Cayman Islands under Toby's name. It was, after all, Toby who was responsible for letting this truth come to light. A young man was evolving before Stan Tress' eyes, making him very proud. Adrienne was, in essence, Toby's partner and whatever the future had in store for them was up in the stars. There was no end in sight as to what these two could accomplish.

This project was the first of a line which would place Toby and Adrienne in high esteem with all of the wildlife on the planet.

To them it was not work, but a labour of love in the creation of this safe haven. Stan and Dixon were invaluable friends. They helped in anyway they could in bringing this idea from the drawing board to its living realization.

It was a success in every sense of the word. To say this kept all involved thoroughly busy was an understatement. Just being there to see what can come true when you believe in an unselfish wish is truly gratifying. This, for the moment, would be the jewel that their commitment would have an infinite endearment.

T
M